FLORISTS' REVIEW   WEDDINGS

2

FLORISTS' REVIEW   WEDDINGS

2

PUBLISHER
Frances Dudley

EXECUTIVE EDITOR
Talmage McLaurin, AIFD

FLORAL DESIGNERS
Talmage McLaurin, AIFD
Bill Harper, AIFD, AAF
James Miller, AIFD

AUTHORS
David Coake and Shelley Urban

ART DIRECTOR AND COPY EDITOR
Michael C. Snell

PROOFREADERS
David Coake and Kelsey Lowe

PRODUCTION COORDINATOR
James Miller, AIFD

PHOTOGRAPHERS
Nathan Ham
Mark Robbins
Stephen Smith
Lon Murdick

Florists' Review Weddings 2 is published by Florists' Review Enterprises, Topeka, Kansas. www.floristsreview.com

Printed in the United States by The John Henry Company, Lansing, Michigan

ISBN 0-9714860-2-6

Florists' Review is the only independent monthly trade magazine for professional florists in the United States. In addition to serving the needs of retail florists through its industry-specific magazine, Florists' Review Enterprises has an active book division that supplies educational products to all who are interested in floral design. For more information, visit our website at www.floristsreview.com.

While a wedding can be as diverse and personal as each couple who enters into its bonds, no celebration of this blessed event seems complete unless flowers are included. Flowers herald the romance that inspired the proposal, enhancing the day's fleeting moments that are remembered nostalgically for years to come.

INTRODUCTION

From traditional, grand ceremonies to small, intimate gatherings to exotic get-away destinations, it's always the flowers that inevitably capture the imagination and become the topic of conversation. And for that all-important day, when everything is held to perfection, the successful presentation of flowers, whether classic or contemporary, results from the careful planning and skill of the floral artist.

Weddings 2, brimming with images from *Florists' Review's* special wedding editions, is a treasury of beautiful photography, astounding blossoms, clever applications, and step-by-step instructional information. It follows our 106-year tradition of showcasing the most loved of all floral-enhanced occasions, the wedding.

C O N T E N T S

STEPHEN SMITH

AMETHYST

AMETHYST PASSIONATE **HEATHER** SPLENDOR **VIOLET** IMPERIAL **PLUM** REGAL **ORCHIDS** RO

MARK ROBBINS

OPPOSITE:
Reflecting natural growth patterns, blushing pink tulips are arranged vertically among a lush "bed" of violet-colored stocks in a floral-foam wreath ring to create a spring garden centerpiece.

MARK ROBBINS

ABOVE:
Sprays of *Dendrobium* orchids have been snipped apart and clustered into a bouquet holder to create this breathtakingly exotic bouquet. The coordinating lei is made from individual florets of the same flowers.

ETHY... ...SSIONATE **HEATHER** SPLENDOR **VIOLET** IMPERIAL **PLUM** REGAL **ORCHIDS** ROYAL

STEPHEN SMITH

LEFT:
This sumptuous ball-shaped bouquet is composed of fragrant 'Lavande' roses and various hues of fresh *Hydrangea* florets ranging from pink and lavender to green. Clusters of pink-headed corsage pins are randomly placed throughout the design to add luxurious detail.

BELOW:
Aranda orchids are hand-tied into a casual yet sophisticated bouquet. Expanding the spotted tropical motif is variegated *Aucuba* (Japanese laurel) foliage, which forms a leafy collar at the base of the exotic blooms.

OPPOSITE:
Traditional hand-tied arm bouquets are again popular with many brides, and they're beautifully appropriate with fuller dress styles—especially when created with flowers in luxurious colors and textures. This glorious design features fully bloomed white *Leptospermum* in combination with monochromatically hued flowers from light-pink *Astilbe* and larkspur to vibrant peonies and *Boronia*, the color of which is repeated in the sumptuous ribbon.

STEPHEN SMITH

OPPOSITE:
Beautifully accessorizing this classic gown is a traditional hand-tied posy of *Scabiosa* blooms and scented geranium foliage, which are arranged through tufts of *Hydrangea* blossoms for support. The foliage was chosen for its color similarity to the luxurious wrap, which is adorned with a scattering of fresh *Delphinium* and *Hydrangea* florets.

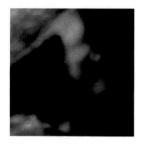

RIGHT:
Silver wire princess baskets are used in both decorative and structural manners for this cake. One basket, with its handle removed, is inverted to create a supporting pillar while a second basket is used to contain an arrangement of 'Bluebird' roses as well as sage, mint, and scented geranium leaves.

STEPHEN SMITH

Cut a piece of plastic foam to fit inside the bottom of a simple satin purse.

RIGHT:
For the totally chic and sleek, nothing complements like these inventive bouquets created in classic, simple satin purses. Easy to carry in a variety of manners, they add an element of glamour and *haute couture* to the event.

Hot-glue the piece of plastic foam into the bottom of the purse.

Hot-glue water picks filled with preservative solution into the plastic foam, and add flowers.

16

how-to
Purse Bouquet

RIGHT:
Spectacular *Cattleya* orchids grace a lush ready-made garland of plumosa fern *(Asparagus)* and nagi *(Podocarpus)*, creating a dramatic floral accessory that can be worn as a boa by daring brides and attendants or carried as a "chain" to link bridesmaids or flower girls. The orchids are secured into the garland with chenille stems.

STEPHEN SMITH

MARK ROBBINS

NATHAN HAM

how-to

Heather Wreath

Make a wreath of fresh
heather by wiring several
pieces of heather together,
in garland fashion, with
thin-gauge paddle wire.

Tie a length of ribbon
onto the wreath, at the
point where the two ends
join, to form a loop handle
by which the wreath can
be carried.

Using floral adhesive, glue
white spray roses into the
wreath at the point where
the ribbon handle is tied.

NATHAN HAM

20

STEPHEN SMITH

LEFT:
This geometric, elongated-teardrop-shaped bouquet is composed of pincushion flowers *(Scabiosa), Delphiniums,* and *Guichenotia.* While traditional cascades are loosely arranged, this updated twist is more dense and sculpted.

RIGHT:
Sleek and sophisticated, this luxurious cascade of blushing lavender *Dendrobium* orchids is a contemporary classic. The mass of blossoms and an absence of foliage contribute to the bouquet's modern, slender look.

LEFT AND RIGHT:
Shaped like a delicious ice-cream cone, this cute and pretty bouquet will win any sweet little girl's heart. Stylish flowers matched with fun shapes might increase younger children's interest in holding on to their flowers during the ceremony.

how-to

Cone Bouquet

23

Bind several stems of heather together at the base of the blooms with thin-gauge wire.

Wrap wire in a spiral fashion down the length of the heather, from the stems to the tips, to form a cone-shaped bunch of heather.

Tie both ends of a length of ribbon to the stem end of the heather cone to form a handle. Then glue spray roses into the stems of the heather to form the top of the bouquet.

MARK ROBBINS

RIGHT:
A pretty and romantic handbag woven of Hawaii's native palm hints of warm, tropical breezes with its collection of budding *Gardenias* and *Cymbidium* florets. The blossoms will withstand warm temperatures best if placed in water tubes.

LEFT:
This design of lisianthuses, *Freesias,* and *Veronica* is the perfect complement for attendants. Created in a silver-handle bouquet holder, the simple but classic styling is stunning against solid and print fabrics alike.

how-to
Orchid Handbag

25

Hot-glue a piece of plastic foam inside an inexpensive handbag, purse, or tote.

Place *Cymbidium* orchids and foliage into water picks.

Apply hot glue to the ends of the orchid-filled water picks, and arrange them in the plastic foam.

A timeless classic with contemporary flair, this elegant nosegay features two varieties of fragrant lavender roses, 'Blue Bird' and 'Sterling Silver,' to create a subtle variation of colors. Tufts of ruffly, gray-green dusty miller, an unexpected but commanding foliage, add a formal garden allure to the bouquet.

RIGHT:
Make the ring-bearer's job even more special by creating a floral pillow fit for a little king. This pillow is edged with 'Million Stars' baby's breath and fresh heather. These flowers are stapled and glued in place, and they will air dry naturally.

how-to
Ring-Bearer Pillow

27

Trim the lace edging from a ring-bearer pillow.

Staple a border of fresh heather around the edge of the pillow.

Glue tufts of 'Million Stars' baby's breath into the edging of heather with floral adhesive.

STEPHEN SMITH

LEFT:
This winning bouquet is designed in two heart-shaped wet foam forms to provide the blossoms with a water source so that wilting will not occur.

RIGHT:
Paperwhites, *Freesias*, and purple statice are combined to form a hand-tied bouquet that is as fragant as it is beautiful. A charming halo of baby's breath completes the look.

how-to
Hydrangea Heart

28

Glue two plastic-backed floral-foam heart forms with waterproof floral adhesive.

Thread a piece of wire through the open nodules at the top of the forms onto which you can tie a ribbon handle.

Arrange fresh *Hydrangea* blossoms into the floral foam, and accent the base with ribbon streamers.

NATHAN HAM

RIGHT:
Beautifully demonstrating how the contrast of deep, rich colors can amplify the allure of spring wedding bouquets, dark reddish-purple "drumstick" *Alliums* and *Freesias* are clustered to form the heart of this texturally exciting hand-tied design.

LEFT:
Although *Irises* are commercially available virtually year-round, they provide a breath of spring whenever they're used. In this charming monobotanical nosegay, *Camellia* leaves are placed throughout the bouquet as well as around the edge, to provide contrast and definition to the *Irises* and to establish a purple and green color harmony.

how-to

Wedding Bow Roll-Ups

31

Using wired woven ribbon, tie a multiloop bow with long, blunt-cut streamers.

Roll the ends of the streamers around a pencil to hide any frayed ends.

Slide the pencil out of each loop, and secure the loop with a dot of hot glue.

LEFT:
Fragrant paperwhite *Narcissi,* along with lavender *Scabiosa* and lisianthuses, are glued into a large multiloop bow to create this fabulous nosegay. A shimmering collection of lightly wired organza ribbons in several spring-time hues form the oversized bow and are excellent choices for this quick-to-make bouquet technique.

OPPOSITE:
A dimensional and striking complementary color harmony is created by arranging sunny yellow 'St. Patrick' roses and yellow-green snowballs *(Viburnum)* amidst flowers in a range of violet hues including pastel *Freesia* blossoms; midrange lilacs *(Syringa)* and onion flowers *(Allium)*; and dark, rich pansies *(Viola)*. A traditional wicker basket is given a more wintry and formal appeal with several dustings of silver spray paint.

how-to
Ribbon Loop Bouquet

Make 12 four-loop bows with several colors of sheer ribbon. Cluster the bows together, and attach their wires to a wooden pick.

Fill a decorative tussie-mussie holder with dry floral foam or plastic foam, and hot-glue the wooden pick on the bow cluster into the foam.

Glue flower blossoms between the loops with floral adhesive until the bouquet takes on the desired size, form, and fullness.

DELFT

DELFT SKY **ETERNAL** OCEAN **TRANQUIL** AZURE **INDIGO** COBALT **PEACEFUL** DENIM **LAPIS** WEDGW

MARK ROBBINS

MARK ROBBINS

LEFT:
This new and long-lasting variation of the stylish pomander bouquet is created by pressing fresh pansies *(Viola)* and *Hydrangea* florets coated with spray adhesive onto a plastic-foam ball. Tasseled cording, inserted through a hole bored in the center of the ball, adds a Victorian touch while creating the handle with which the bouquet is carried.

OPPOSITE:
Because matching blues is always a challenge—and probably not the best choice anyway—blending a variety of blues, and even lavenders, is an ideal alternative. This glorious hand-tied arm bouquet of Pacific Hybrid (or Elatum) *Delphiniums* will beautifully coordinate with virtually any blue gown.

STEPHEN SMITH

STEPHEN SMITH

how-to
Couture Wrap Nosegay

OPPOSITE AND RIGHT:
Nestled into a neatly clipped, dense cluster of baby's breath *(Gypsophila),* a distinctive combination of gardeny blossoms in blue-violet and lavender form a contemporary nosegay for sophisticated fall and winter brides.

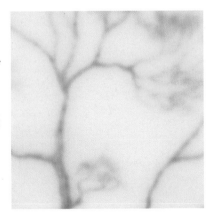

Remove the lower branches from a full bunch of baby's breath, and bundle all the blooms tightly into a dense nosegay. Bind with water-proof tape. Trim the baby's breath to create a flat top.

Wrap feathery ribbon around the perimeter of the flat-topped bundle of baby's breath. Then tuck in stems of lily grass *(Liriope),* and wrap them randomly around the edge of the bouquet.

Glue *Ageratum, Agapanthus,* and *Eryngium* blossoms into the baby's breath bundle with floral adhesive. Then glue stems of *Veronica* around the edge of the bouquet. Wrap the stem handle with ribbon.

NATHAN HAM

how-to

Floral Purse

40

Cover the exterior of a chipwood box with fresh ivy leaves, gluing them in place with spray adhesive.

Glue one piece of *Liriope* to each side of the box, then overlap the tips of the two pieces above the box, and secure them together with floral adhesive, forming a handle.

Glue tufts of 'Million Stars' baby's breath into the box so that it protrudes just from the top, then glue individual *Agapanthus* florets into the tufts of baby's breath.

NATHAN HAM

BELOW:
Delphinium florets are combined with pineapple mint leaves for a fresh and colorful summer creation.

MARK ROBBINS

OPPOSITE AND ABOVE RIGHT:
This romantic nosegay, abundant with delicate pale blue *Agapanthus* blossoms and lavender *Freesias,* resembles the modern style of monobotanical compositions. The thoughtfully chosen, nearly monochromatic collection of blooms, backed with *Hydrangea* leaves, is densely constructed using hand tying, gluing, and wiring and taping techniques.

STEPHEN SMITH

how-to
Lavender Clutch Nosegay

43

Cluster several stems of *Agapanthuses* to form a bouquet of the desired size. Bind the stems just below the blossoms with green waterproof tape.

Glue *Freesia* blooms with 2-inch to 3-inch stems into the cluster of *Agapanthuses* with floral adhesive.

Using green waterproof tape, bind wired *Hydrangea* leaves to the underside of the bouquet to form a foliage collar around the bouquet.

STEPHEN SMITH

LEFT AND OPPOSITE:
For the bride who wants something totally innovative yet romantic, something contemporary yet Victorian inspired, this sensational parasol-shaped creation of fresh pansy blooms and *Hydrangea* florets should do the trick. The delicate blossoms are glued to both the top and underside of a silver woven wire "dome," which is fashioned from a metal princess basket.

how-to

Mosaic Petals Bouquet

44

BELOW:
Agapanthus florets and mint *(Mentha)* leaves.

Cut off the handle of a silver wire princess basket. Then cut out the bottom of the basket, too. Bend the upward curved rim of the basket so that it curves downward, like a parasol.

Replace the floral foam in a bouquet holder with a disk of plastic foam. Insert the holder into the reshaped wire basket. Squeeze the wire around the handle, and hot-glue into a tussie-mussie holder.

Spray fresh *Hydrangea* and pansy blooms with adhesive, and randomly place them on the top and underside of the wire "parasol," making sure the center is completely covered.

STEPHEN SMITH

MARK ROBBINS

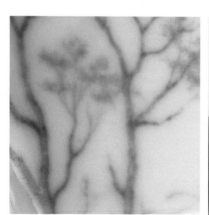

NATHAN HAM

LEFT AND OPPOSITE:
Yellow tulips are combined with blue *Anemones*, sea holly *(Eryngium)*, lady's mantle *(Alchemilla)*, *Clematis*, hyacinths, and more to form a vibrant complementary color harmony that is stunning for fall. A feathery fringe adds warmth and dimension to the composition.

LEFT:

A simple but extravagant hand-tied profusion of grape hyacinths *(Muscari)*, edged with orange jessamine *(Murraya)* foliage, is the quintessential spring bouquet—round and modest in size, with premium blooms and a gardeny appeal. The coordinating boutonniere, fashioned of five grape hyacinth blooms, is decoratively bound at a single point with silver beading wire. Short lengths of wire are inserted into the stems for added durability.

SHELL

SHELL BLUSH **INNOCENT** POWDER **SOFT** FEMININE **TENDER** PETAL **TIMID** BUFF **APPLE BLOS**

Carrying the elegant
detailing of pearl-studded
ribbon into the flowers,
pearl white pear-head
corsage pins are pushed
into the roses—single
pins in unopened buds
and clusters of pins in
opened blooms. The pins
are dipped into floral
adhesive before being
inserted into the roses.

LL BLUSH **INNOCENT** POWDER **SOFT** FEMININE **TENDER** PETAL **TIMID** BUFF **APPLE BLOSSOM**

STEPHEN SMITH

STEPHEN SMITH

LEFT:

A silky, semi-transparent ribbon is woven among the pale peach 'Osiana' rose blossoms that compose this monobotanical nosegay. The wide, wire-edged ribbon is complemented by pearl-headed corsage pins that not only decorate the ribbon wrapping but help to secure it in place. To finish the bouquet, long streamers of the ribbon, which has a subtly crinkled texture, are added.

how-to
Ribbon Collars for Roses

52

Fold extra-wide wired ribbon in half lengthwise with the two wired edges together. Gather the ribbon from both ends into the center. Twist the wire ends together.

Place one rose through the center hole in each collar so that the collars envelop the roses.

Arrange the ribbon-collared roses into a floral-foam bouquet holder. Insert clusters of pearl-head corsage pins into the ribbon randomly throughout the bouquet.

MARK ROBBINS

ABOVE:

Sprigs of berried juniper (*Juniperus spp.*) are the perfect winter wedding accent to beautiful 'Pocelina' rose blooms.

Two varieties of blush roses—'Sahara' and 'Porcelina'—are combined in this grand mound-shaped bouquet.

STEPHEN SMITH

OPPOSITE AND RIGHT:
Designed in a straight-handle bouquet holder, this free-form cluster of white 'Akito' hybrid tea roses and blush-white 'Porcelina' spray rose buds is given a distinctive, cascade-like flair with exotic pheasant feathers, which protrude from a hole in the bottom of the bouquet holder handle.

STEPHEN SMITH

55

RIGHT:
Elegant cake serving pieces deserve a decorative touch on the special day, and these adornments are simple and quick to create. The bows of ivory pleated organza ribbon are made and tied onto the servers first. Then the roses are glued at the last minute into the center of the bows with floral adhesive.

STEPHEN SMITH

These plain pumps are given a high-fashion treatment with luxurious ribbon and fresh miniature carnations, sure to cause lots of favorable comments.

how-to
Shoe Adornment

56

Using double-faced ribbon, make a "ribbon candy"-style bow with four loops on each side, without scrunching or twisting the ribbon in the center. Secure the bow by stapling through the center.

Affix the bow to the shoe with hot glue. You can also staple the bow to the shoe, but make sure that the staple ends are on the outside of the shoe.

Hold a miniature carnation by the petals, and cut off the calyx. Apply floral adhesive to the base of the petals, and press them onto the center of the bow.

ABOVE:
Among true style setters, diminutive round bouquets are the popular choice, even for brides. For them, bouquets are regarded as accessories. And when the florals—like these delicate pink roses and glossy foliage—are placed into elegant silver posy holders, the epitome of modern style is created.

OPPOSITE:
The pretty petals from several tulip-shaped 'Charming Unique' roses form this stunning cup-shaped design. Silver-painted *Magnolia* leaves, arranged backside up, beautifully accent the fabulous duchess rose.

LEFT:
For your upcoming wedding receptions and parties, dazzle your customers and their guests with this clever idea for accessorizing votive candleholders. The glass candleholders are wrapped with #40-width satin ribbon to provide diffused light similar to a frosted holder.

how-to
Tulip Votives

58

Gently reflex the petals of a French tulip. Remove the pistils and stamens with a knife. Cut off the stem flush with the base of the bloom.

Cut a length of ribbon, and wrap it around a straight-sided glass votive candleholder. Secure with hot glue.

Set the glass votive holder into the center of the tulip. Curve the petals back to their natural positions to "cup" the votive holder.

ABOVE:
Perfect for a couple who desires a soft and simple yet elegant holiday wedding motif, this floral badge of cream-colored spray roses features a Christmas star ornament. The flowers are arranged in a foam cage and set into the center of a double-loop gold mesh bow, with streamers cascading from the design.

The sandy hues of 'Sahara de Meilland' roses are beautifully accented for autumn nuptials with a mix of fall foliages, immature grapes, and natural grape vines. The flowing vines join the sophisticated arrangement with the tabletop elements, the most notable of which are hens and chicks (Echeveria).

FLAMINGO

FLAMINGO SPIRITED **BUBBLE GUM** BUBBLY **FUCHSIA** COTTON CANDY *GIRLY* ROSE **AZALEA** HEAL

RIGHT:
Created as a tropical composite flower, this nosegay is assembled with a jester *Protea (Protea obtusifolia)* and red and purple Amnicola *Anthuriums*, which have had their spadices removed. A collar of burgundy-edge *Dracaena* leaves completes the vibrant complementary color harmony.

MARK ROBBINS

MINGO SPIRITED **BUBBLE GUM** BUBBLY *FUCHSIA* COTTON CANDY **GIRLY** ROSE **AZALEA** HEALTHY

OPPOSITE:
For a modern cascade-style bouquet, tulips are an ideal choice. Capitalizing on the natural curvature of their stems, these beautiful bicolor 'Lucky Strike' tulips are hand-tied into an elongated bouquet, then placed into a vase and draped with a damp hand towel to maintain the bouquet's natural cascading shape.

STEPHEN SMITH

LEFT:
A hot-pink velvet ribbon helps set a holiday tone for a romantic spray-rose-covered heart. Buds are intermixed throughout the design for added interest.

A successful blend of femininity, romance, and regalness, this innovative columnar composition exclusively showcases *Cymbidium* orchids in blush pink and rich burgundy colorings. Using blossoms with long wired-and-taped "stems," the all-sided bouquet is assembled, beginning at the bottom, by adding one bloom at a time. The stem of each successively placed bloom is wrapped in a spiral fashion around the central stem of wire.

RIGHT:

What could be more glamorous and exciting than an accent of exotic soft-pink marabou feathers? Having both a contemporary and a retro flair, the soft-pink feathers are an ideal "bridge" between the creamy white and pinkish-red bicolor roses and the white bridal gown, and they festively finish the underside of the bouquet. Perfectly sized for bouquets, small marabou feather boas are available at craft and toy stores.

how-to
Feather-Edged Nosegay

Arrange roses into a nosegay in your hands, and secure the stems with waterproof tape.

Secure a mini feather boa to the top of the handle, and coil it around the underside of the bouquet.

To hold the feather boa in place, push corsage pins through the boa into the calyxes or stems of the roses.

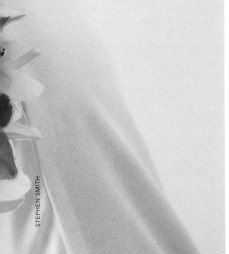

MARK ROBBINS

RIGHT AND ABOVE RIGHT:
As tenderly romantic and
feminine as antique lace,
this sumputous collection
of blush pink 'Emma'
roses and bright white
Freesias is the essence
of modern sophistication
but with an influence of
vintage Victorian.

OPPOSITE AND ABOVE LEFT:
This exquisite monotone
nosegay of raspberry
pink 'Orlando' roses
and 'Rossini' *Freesias* is
a lovely complement
for bridesmaids.

how-to
Leaf-Wrapped Roses

68

Using roses that are stripped of thorns and foliage, wrap two or three *Galax* leaves around each bloom.

Using thin-guage wire, pierce through the bottom portion of the leaves, just below the rose bloom, to secure the cone shape.

Form a "vine wreath" to encircle the bouquet using ivy stems stripped of their leaves and lengths of wire covered in stem wrap to match the ivy stems.

LEFT:

There is more than one way to accent a bouquet with foliage, and in this modern hand-tied design, each rose is encased in a pair of *Galax* leaves prior to assembly. The leaves are wrapped around the roses, in a conical fashion, and taped to the foliage-stripped rose stems just underneath the blooms.

RIGHT:

A riot of colors and patterns is created by combining exotically marked hybrid orchids, including *Odontoglossum*, *Miltonia*, and *Paphiopedilum* (lady's slipper), with vibrantly colored *Cattleya*, *Phalaenopsis* (moth orchid), and *Cymbidium* hybrids into a singular bouquet. Variagated *Aucuba* (Japanese spotted laurel) foliage adds another dimension to the mix of colors and patterns.

OPPOSITE:
Forming a vibrant, festive color harmony and creating an English garden spirit, fresh *Hydrangeas* in variations of green are assimilated in a contrasting harmony with hybrid tea roses—including 'Yves Piaget,' an English rose look-alike—and *Freesias* in a range of hot-pink hues.

BELOW:
Waiting to begin her journey down the aisle, this charming flower girl will carry a wreath-shaped bouquet of fragrant white *Stephanotis* blossoms, soft-pink roses, and scented geranium leaves. This delightful, symbolic bouquet style is almost foolproof for a young girl to carry because the wreath appears perfect regardless of the way she holds it.

RIGHT:
A most unusual and charming flower girl "bouquet," this cuddly teddy bear is one she'll be happy to hold. Sporting a collar of fresh flowers, the furry friend is sure to calm even the most anxious child as well as bring smiles to the guests' faces.

MARK ROBBINS

MARK ROBBINS

how-to
Teddy Bear Bouquet

71

Tie a length of ribbon around the neck of a plush teddy bear.

Trim excess ribbon, leaving short tails.

Glue fresh flowers to the ribbon with floral adhesive.

STEPHEN SMITH

OPPOSITE:
Delicately redolent, apricot-hued 'Evelyn' English roses combine with pristine white lilies-of-the-valley, *Freesias*, and *Hyacinths* to create a sensory delight for both the nose and the eyes.

LEFT:
This lovely traditionally styled bridal nosegay, enhanced with a bow and streamers of satin ribbon, is composed of pretty pink 'Saphir' roses arranged in a bouquet holder.

BELOW:
Especially appropriate for a bridesmaid or flower girl, this romantic, fragrant heart-shaped bouquet comprises two soft-hued varieties of pink spray roses. The roses are wired and taped, making it easier to arrange them into the heart shape. Salal leaves, also wired and taped, are trimmed with scissors and edged with pink rose petals to finish the backside of the bouquet and further define the shape.

how-to

Doily Collars

Cut a small hole in the center of a crocheted lace doily, insert a rose stem through the hole, and slide the doily up the stem and over the calyx to the base of the bloom.

MARK ROBBINS

STEPHEN SMITH

The luxurious satin-and-button-covered handle of this sophisticated carnation nosegay is created by wrapping the long, foliage-free stems first with stem wrap, to create a smooth surface, and then with a beautiful satin ribbon. Satin-covered buttons are hot-glued after the tiny metal thread loops are snipped from the backsides of the buttons.

OPPOSITE:
Pastel pink miniature *Gerberas* are dressed up for any springtime event with the addition of this playful banded ribbon. When wrapped around the flowers' stems, the ribbon's banded edge yields a decorative striped appearance, offering an up-to-date treatment.

how-to
Carnation Candlesticks

Cut carnation stems short, and arrange them into 4½-inch-diameter floral-foam spheres, leaving a small space for the sphere to be placed onto the candlestick.

OPPOSITE:
Densely clustered in the center of this grand bouquet, blushing tulips are distinctively paired with miniature *Cymbidium* orchids to create a classic yet contemporary statement. Although the two types of flowers have similar colorings, the mass of smooth, tightly closed tulips provides contrast in both texture and form to the border of ruffly, spotted orchids. Modern classicism is further carried out with the elegant, intricately detailed handle of the bouquet holder.

STEPHEN SMITH

LEFT:
This reception design of standard pink carnation-covered floral-foam spheres and silver candlesticks mixes contemporary, lush, and geometric florals with traditional silver pieces. The true charm of this design lies in the mix-and-match silver candlesticks, so the look is perfect for incorporating silver rental pieces with family heirlooms. To secure the floral-foam spheres to the candlesticks, place a short candle into each holder to act as a "spike" on which the sphere can rest.

ABOVE:
The deep, rich hues of chocolate mint leaves are gorgeous embellishments for soft-colored 'Majolica' spray roses.

LEFT AND OPPOSITE:
Clustered in a spherical topiary style, two varieties of pink Guernsey lilies (*Nerines*) form coordinating fluffy nosegays for brides and maids. The simple styling is easily achieved by binding the stems just beneath the blooms with waterproof tape, which is then covered with a band of luxurious ribbon.

LEFT:
Ribbon adds an elegant
finish to men's flowers
for formal occasions, and
a couple of diagonal-cut
ribbon "tails" are hand-
some alternatives to
decorative foliage.

BELOW:
Cone-shaped baskets of
hammered silver metal,
inspired by Victorian
Christmas tree adornments,
are perfectly suited for
dainty flower-girl bouquets
as well as guest favors
containing petals with which
to shower the newlyweds
as they depart.

how-to
Ribbon-Wrapped Boutonniere

80

Cut a rose stem to 3
inches in length. Wire
the stem, and tape it with
light-green stem wrap.

Fold a length of No. 9-
width ribbon in half
lengthwise. Wrap the rose
stem with the ribbon from
the top down to the end
and then back up. Secure
with a straight pin.

Tie a piece of ribbon
around the top of the
stem, just beneath
the bloom, to conceal
the pin. Cut the ribbon
ends to leave short
decorative "tails."

Two colors of luxurious moiré ribbon are laid back to back and tied into a bow to form a stunning accent for the hand-tied bouquet featuring sweet-smelling stocks *(Matthiola)* and frosted, crystal-like, flower-shaped buttons with gold centers.

how-to
Tropical Fan Bouquet

83

LEFT AND ABOVE RIGHT:
To create this fan-style bouquet with a flair for the Far East, tips of 'Sexy Pink' *Heliconias* are backed by broad, yellow-edge ti leaves. Another layer of red-tip ti leaves enhances the color on the front of the fan, while short rows of ginger *(Alpinia)* tips and *Cymbidium* orchids embellish the base.

Wire and tape the tips of five or six 'Sexy Pink' *Heliconias*. Using a heavy-gauge wire, "sew" the tips together in a fan shape.

Using spray adhesive, attach ti leaves to the back of the *Heliconia*-tip "fan." Tape the stems of the leaves together at the bottom of the "fan."

Glue another row of smaller ti leaves to the front of the *Heliconia* tips. Tape wired ginger tips and orchids at the base of the "fan." Wrap the handle with ribbon.

LIPSTICK

LIPSTICK CHERRY **SEDUCTIVE** VALENTINE **SCARLET** ROUGE **EXCITING** CRIMSON **HOT** CARDINAL **RUBY** B

MARK ROBBINS

OPPOSITE:
The quintessential bouquet for modern winter weddings, this circular sensation comprises a mass of reddish *Hypericum* berries "ringed" with fragrant green cedar. Such understated beauty is just what's called for in today's refined, elegant ceremonies.

BELOW:
At the focal point of this design, arranged in a moss-lined rusted iron basket, is an eye-catching mass of sumptuous roses, made by placing the florals in a pavé manner into a floral-foam sphere. Accenting the rose orb is a mixture of holiday greens, berried branches, dusty miller, and lily grass (*Liriope*).

TICK CHERRY **SEDUCTIVE** VALENTINE **SCARLET** ROUGE EXCITING CRIMSON **HOT** CARDINAL **RUBY** BERRY

STEPHEN SMITH

LEFT:
'Nicole' roses placed at different heights create the illusion of depth, floating above a fluffy collar of ribbon, which conveniently hides the bouquet holder and gives the stylish look of a hand-tied design. The crisp red-and-silver ribbon, tied into multiloop bows, is attached through holes on the back of the bouquet holder.

BELOW AND OPPOSITE:
Replicating the feeling of a late summer garden in this casual but lush seasonal bouquet, spikes of red *Leptospermum* and clusters of *Hypericum* berries create a "thicket" of filler materials into which bright scarlet red 'Kardinal' roses and fragrant lavender 'Bluebird' roses are arranged. Petal-free *Gerbera* centers are also included as an unexpected botanical element.

how-to

Ribbon-Collared Bouquet

Tie several six- to eight-loop bows of metallic wired ribbon.

Insert one bow into each opening on the back of a straight-handle bouquet holder.

Fluff the bows into a uniform collar. Add roses to finish the design.

LEFT:
Especially lovely for evening ceremonies, candlelit attendants' bouquets provide a warm, romantic ambience. Inspired by the Biedermeier style of flower arrangement, the concentric rings of florals in the bouquet represent a rich harmony of analogous colors.

MARK ROBBINS

OPPOSITE:
Lush cake enhancements celebrate the bounty and beauty of autumn. At the base, a glorious gathering of materials, including roses, orchids, sea holly (*Eryngium*), *Hypericum* berries, key limes, and fall leaves, is secured into a floral-foam wreath ring, and the cake stand is simply placed into the center of the tabletop wreath.

how-to
Hurricane Candle Bouquet

90

Trim off the bottom portion of a straight-handle bouquet holder. Hot-glue the remaining length of handle into a silver posy holder.

Clip away the top of the bouquet holder's plastic cage. Re-secure the floral foam into the holder with hot glue, if necessary.

MARK ROBBINS

Hot-glue a glass hurricane globe securely into the center of the foam. Add a candle and flowers.

ABOVE:
Cinnamon-scented geranium leaves are a wonderful complement to this holiday-inspired boutonniere, which features a 'Nelson' carnation and holly berries and foliage.

LEFT AND OPPOSITE:
Comprising vibrant orange *Nerines,* golden auburn *Hypericum* berries, and sunny yellow *Bupleurum,* this hand-tied mass bouquet embodies the colors of fall. The interplay of textures among the three materials lends important visual interest to the simple construction.

92

RIGHT:
An exquisite offering for Christmastime weddings, this striking centerpiece is created in two parts. First, a vase of various fruits is filled with club soda, giving the fruit a beaded appearance. Then, a foam-filled bowl, into which the florals are arranged, is placed atop the vase. Velvety red roses, dusty miller, berried juniper, and pine branches are a captivating combination for this holiday wedding design.

POLAR

POLAR IVORY **FROST** DOVE **SNOW** PURE **OPAL** PEARL **CLEAN** WINTER **CLOUD** BISQUE **GARDENIA**

Fluffy white *Irises*, the long stems of which are decoratively bound with elegant sheer ribbon, are massed to create an almost scepter-like bouquet with a formal yet gardeny appeal. The absence of foliage intensifies the bouquet's contemporary flair.

MARK ROBBINS

ABOVE:
A free-form gathering of fragrant, pure white Easter lilies *(Lilium longi-florum),* hand-tied into an impressive yet manageable bouquet, exemplifies the simplicity found in even the grandest of today's bridal flowers.

LEFT:
Cattleyas are the archetypal glamorous orchids, and with frilled petal edges and showy colored labella (lips), they yearn to be presented simply and elegantly. In this bouquet, three exquisite blossoms and a few shiny, dark-green *Camellia* leaves are casually arranged in a straight-handle bouquet holder with the foam cage hidden beneath "swirls" of bear grass.

98

RIGHT:
With today's trend toward simple bouquets designed with special flowers, this clutch of extravagant *Cattleya* orchids is on the cutting edge. Enhanced by salal leaves, this exquisite bouquet is small but lush and very special.

OPPOSITE:
Leafless stems of miniature bloom 'Million Stars' baby's breath are densely gathered in layers to form this very vogue, cloud-like bouquet.

Accentuating this bouquet's casual yet elegant spring garden appeal is a lush, fluffy edging of variegated *Pittosporum tenuifolium*, a popular species, that is native to New Zealand and commonly known as kohuhu.

NATHAN HAM

LEFT:
A collection of small four-loop bows, made from two translucent wired ribbons, form a fluffy collar into which a tightly massed grouping of exquisite white moth orchids *(Phalaenopsis)* is nestled.

101

ABOVE:
Random splashes of color are introduced into this sumptuous nosegay of white stocks *(Matthiola)* with light-blue *Delphinium* Belladonna blooms and pieces of green bells-of-Ireland *(Moluccella).*

White roses, a standard for weddings year-round, assume a wintry feeling when accented with sprigs of pine. And when arranged in a captivating conical shape—almost Christmas tree-like—a striking bouquet is created. This hand-tied design of 'Escimo' roses is enchantingly accessorized with narrow black goose feathers, which are tied on silver beading wire and woven amidst the roses.

RIGHT:
Although the traditional use of corsages for weddings seems to be on the decline in recent years, the boutonniere, like this cluster of *Freesia* blossoms, remains a fashion staple for the men in the wedding party.

STEPHEN SMITH

NATHAN HAM

103

ABOVE:
While multiple-bloom boutonnieres often look like small corsages, this simple gathering of diminutive *Stephanotis* blossoms creates a refined, understated groom's boutonniere.

MARK ROBBINS

LEFT:
For an impressive finishing touch to the groom's attire, this boutonniere of paperwhite *Narcissi*, embellished by the handsome variegated leaves of Swedish ivy *(Plectranthrus australis),* is an outstanding selection.

BELOW LEFT:
Rose-scented geranium leaves, an unexpected addition to the cluster of lilies-of-the-valley, help to transform the delicate blossoms into a handsome buttonhole arrangement.

MARK ROBBINS

STEPHEN SMITH

LEFT:
Elegant silver tussie-mussie holders and opulent silk tassels—both fashionable and luxurious ornaments—are naturals for combining when bouquets of distinction and grand style are the goal. The adornment of this simple silver tussie-mussie holder with an ivory tassel, specifically selected to complement the cream-colored roses and off-white *Bouvardia*, creates a spectacular bouquet handle.

how-to
Tasseled Tussie-Mussie

104

Hot-glue a decorative tassel to the bottom of a simple metal or plastic tussie-mussie holder.

METHOD 1. Bouquet holder: Hot-glue a straight-handle bouquet holder into the tussie-mussie, and arrange flowers.

METHOD 2. Hand-tied bouquet: Arrange flowers in your hand and, when finished, insert the stems into the tussie-mussie holder.

RIGHT:
A traditional nosegay of beautifully opening, diamond-white 'Escimo' roses is given an unexpected opulence with the incorporation of sparkling crystal buttons in the center of variegated *Pittosporum* "rosettes."

MARK ROBBINS

OPPOSITE AND ABOVE:
Considered the quintes-
sential wedding flowers—
and the fifth thing brides
should carry (right after
something old, something
new, etc.)—lilies-of-the-
valley impart a sophisiti-
cation and elegance that
is unachievable with
almost any other flowers.
Here, a sumptuous
gathering of the sweetly
fragrant flowers is simply
and tastefully designed
in a silver tussie-mussie
holder, providing the
ultimate in refinement
and style. For equally
opulent centerpieces,
Chinese porcelain planters
are filled with cut lilies-of-
the-valley arranged to
mimic potted plantings.
Unbeknownst to many,
lilies-of-the-valley are
available year-round from
select specialty flower
growers, provided that
the growers are given at
least six weeks notice and
that customers are willing
to pay the price.

FERN

FERN YOUNG GRASS FRESH EMERALD LUSH LIME MOSS PINE FOREST BASIL BAMBOO LEAF VERD

OPPOSITE:
Beautifully imparting the ambience of autumn, the fresh wheat surrounding this all-white bouquet provides a distinctive edge to the design. The flowers—'Akito' roses, *Stephanotises*, and lisianthuses—are arranged in a straight-handle bouquet holder, which is nestled into the center of the bundle of wheat, splaying the heads into a circular base.

RIGHT:
In addition to being arranged into a small floral-foam cage, wheat covers the "columns" between the layers of this three-tiered cake. Freeze-dried gourds, with soft, dusty looks and in various shapes, sizes, and textures, are placed sporadically around the cake layers and at the base.

STEPHEN SMITH

OPPOSITE:
This voguish bouquet of nearly neutral-colored *Hydrangeas, Ageratums,* and grapes is a distinctive selection for autumn and winter nuptials. With its dusty greens, blues, and lavenders, it has virtually unlimited versatility and will beautifully accent dresses of almost any hue.

BELOW:
An abstract formation of green 'Midori' *Anthuriums* makes a dramatic presentation that would beautifully coordinate with pale pastel-colored bridesmaids' dresses, especially those in the yellow hues.

RIGHT:
Giving this bouquet a distinctive, fluffy edge, fresh millet *(Setaria)* surrounds a neutral collection of *Dahlias,* spray chrysanthemums, and *Hypericum* berries. The flowers are arranged into a straight-handled bouquet holder, which is nestled into the center of the bundle of millet.

Millet Sheaf

113

Bundle several bunches of millet, and bind them just beneath the heads with green waterproof tape.

Tape the straight handle of a bouquet holder with green stem wrap. Glue the holder into the center of the bundle of millet with floral adhesive.

Arrange flowers in the bouquet holder, and finish by adding a few stems of millet into the center of the design.

LEFT:
This fresh bouquet gets a summery citrus "flavor" with a combination of striking yellowish-green 'Limona' roses and limy green *Hypericum* berries. Umbrella fern, an unusual foliage that's native to Australia, gives the bouquet a feathery, star-like form. The bouquet is designed in a straight-handled holder that is beautifully camouflaged inside an elegant, cone-shaped, fabric-covered holder, commercially known as a Posy Pocket. A beautiful silver stand provides a gracious method for displaying the bouquet.

RIGHT:
Nestled into tufts of fresh green *Hydrangea* blossoms, chartreuse *Cymbidium* orchids with contrasting burgundy spotted labella are presented in a fashionable hand-tied bouquet. The orchid stems, which are wired and taped, are inserted through the mass of *Hydrangeas,* and all stems are bound just beneath the flower heads with green waterproof tape. A Dior-style bow of elegant chartreuse satin ribbon finishes the bouquet and hides the taped binding point.

RIGHT:

In this striking yellowish-green and white bouquet, FloraLock™ is used to seal stems of *Cymbidium* orchids, goldenrod *(Solidago)*, spray chrysanthemums, and *Stephanotises* into a bouquet holder. Burgundy and silver wire swirl decoratively around the flowers, their colors respectively picking up the markings on the orchids and accenting the silver bouquet holder.

how-to
Secure and Stable Bouquets

Arrange flowers in a foam-filled bouquet holder, then spray FloraLock™ Stem Adhesive onto the insertion points using the spray straw.

Classically elegant with
an exotic inclination, this
extraordinary nosegay
showcases an outstanding
pairing of tropical Amazon
lilies *(Eucharis)* and unusual
'Lemon Lime' amaryllises
(Hippeastrum). Natives
of Colombia and Peru,
the icy-white, delicately
fragrant Amazon lilies
have pale green centers
that are an exquisite
reflection of the novel hue
of the amaryllises.

LEFT:
Although beautiful
chartreuse *Dendrobium*
orchids lend a formal feel,
the spiky form of citrus-
scented geranium leaves
adds a casual touch,
making this boutonniere
appropriate for either
day or evening events.

MARK ROBBINS

BELOW:
An interesting combina-
tion of flowers, foliages,
candles, and containers,
in different shades of
green, makes a natural
buffet design. A bundle
crafted from myrtle and
rosemary lends a sheaf-like
appearance to a contem-
porary square-based
candelabrum.

how-to

A Natural Candelabrum

117

STEPHEN SMITH

Using myrtle and rosemary,
create a sheaf of greenery
around a candelabrum.
Secure the bottom with a
wrapping of wire.

LEMON

LEMON SUNSHINE **DAFFODIL** SAFFRON **ENERGETIC** BUTTER **CITRON** BLOND **HAPPY** CANARY **CADMIUM**

RIGHT:
Giving this exquisite nosegay great bridal style are white *Cattleya* orchids with yellow labella, which are surrounded by golden yellow *Cymbidium* and *Odontoglossum* hybrid orchids with dramatic burgundy markings.

OPPOSITE:
This voluptuous composition of English roses appears to have a rather haphazard, unplanned placement of colors, emphasizing its "garden picked" appeal. The casual styling is equally achievable by arranging the flowers into a bouquet holder, as is done in this example, or by hand tying.

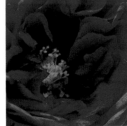

LEFT AND ABOVE RIGHT:
Shower the bride in exotic blossoms with this exquisite parasol, which is constructed with literally hundreds of dancing lady *(Oncidium)* orchids. A beehive ginger *(Zingiber spectabilis)* blossom tops off this dazzling creation while ti leaves and a discarded *Heliconia* stem support the design.

how-to
Orchid Parasol

123

Use a straight-handled bouquet holder, or straighten the handle of a flat-handle bouquet holder by heating it with a flame. Slice through the top few inches of a *Heliconia* or ginger stem, and hot-glue the bouquet holder handle into the stem.

Wrap the top of the stem with stem wrap to cover the sliced area. Glue a row of ti leaves to the stem to cover the bottom of the bouquet holder.

Arrange *Oncidium* orchids in a flat, circular placement to form the parasol. Add a beehive ginger blossom and foliage to the center of the bouquet holder to cover any exposed floral foam.

how-to
Ribbon-Striped Stems

Bundle permanent *Equisetum,* and bind the ends with tape. Tie pieces of No.16-width ribbon individually around the bundle. Knot each piece.

Glue *Galax* leaves to the base of a bouquet holder with spray adhesive. Insert the bouquet holder into the center of the bundle of stems.

Arrange flowers and foliages of choice into the bouquet holder.

LEFT AND OPPOSITE: A trio of ribbons in olive, basil, and yellow, are tied in individual strips to create an unusually captivating striped handle treatment for a sunny gathering of 'Limona' roses, miniature callas, *Ranunculuses,* and seeded *Eucalyptus.*

BELOW: Tucked into a cluster of golden kangaroo paws *(Anigozanthos),* bits of rosemary enhance the masculinity of these appealing boutonnieres.

ABOVE:
Sunny yellow and white *Freesia* blooms, along with snippets of baby's breath *(Gypsophila),* are accented by a few sprigs of lemon *Verbena* and lemon balm to create this pleasingly fragrant design.

how-to
Geometric Collar

Coat the inside of a round plastic liner with aerosol leaf shine. Cut bear grass into 3-inch to 4-inch pieces, and sprinkle them into the liner, spraying lightly with adhesive as you sprinkle. Shape the sticky clippings into a "disc."

Insert the bouquet holder handle through the "disc" of bear-grass clippings. Glue the "disc" to the bottom of the bouquet holder with liquid adhesive.

OPPOSITE AND ABOVE RIGHT:
With its coarse textures and hard geometric lines, a collar of clipped bear grass serves as a striking backdrop that enables the serene gathering of smooth-petaled miniature callas and orchids to shine brightly.

Wrap the handle of a straight-handle bouquet holder with waterproof tape, sticky side out. Press full-length stems of bear grass onto the handle. Finish the top of the handle with ribbon wrap.

AMBER

AMBER WARM **CANDLELIGHT** GLOW **GOLDEN** RICH **CARAMEL** COGNAC **HONEY** TOPAZ **CASHMERE** G

MARK ROBBINS

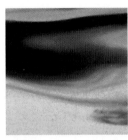

ABOVE AND BELOW:
The refreshing
sorbet-like hues
of apricot-colored
'Sari' roses and
tangerine carnations
produce a deliciously
summery nosegay.

ER WARM **CANDLELIGHT** GLOW **GOLDEN** RICH **CARAMEL** COGNAC **HONEY** TOPAZ **CASHMERE** GLOW

OPPOSITE:
Delicately scented
Stephanotises and diminutive mandarin oranges
combine to create a
tropical-inspired bouquet
for brides who want
something delightful and
different. With all materials
wired and taped, includ-
ing the fruit, this nosegay
is easily hand tied, but it
can also be designed in a
bouquet holder.

NATHAN HAM

RIGHT:
Several beehive ginger (*Zingiber spectabilis*) blossoms give this rare clutch bouquet its exotic quality. Accented by delicate *Cymbidium* orchid florets and tightly nestled clusters of *Hypericum* berries (St. John's wort), the bouquet has an earthy, tropical appeal.

133

OPPOSITE:
Featuring bird-of-paradise (*Strelitzia reginae*) florets, this vibrantly colored bouquet is crafted using the old-fashioned wire-and-tape method. The spiky shapes of the blooms along with exotic foliage enhancements yields an audacious arrangement for the radiant bride.

LEFT:
Wonderfully wild, this exotic-looking clutch bouquet features a large cut-leaf *Banksia* accented by two woolly orange *Banksias* and a pincushion (*Leucospermum*). Nestled amid the unrefined-looking blooms are the very charming blossoms of *Stephanotis*.

RIGHT:
The apricot color of 'Sari' roses makes this bouquet an exquisite choice for fall weddings, and the coordinating satin ribbon treatment at its base provides a comfortable and clean place to hold the bouquet as well as a contemporary and professional finish.

STEPHEN SMITH

how-to
Torch Bouquet

135

OPPOSITE:
This contemporary styling of diminutive callas, which are wired and taped, takes on a European inspiration with the encircling pliable green vines that surround the florals. Several pieces of vine are woven around and through the bouquet to create the modern, natural design.

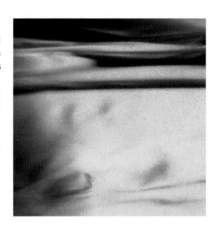

Strip leaves from the bottom few inches of several stems of myrtle. Gather the stems, and bind them into a bundle just below the leaves at the top of the bare stems.

Apply hot glue to the end of a medium-size straight-handle bouquet holder, and nestle it into the center of the myrtle cluster until the end of the handle meets the binding point.

Arrange roses into the bouquet holder to extend just above the tops of the myrtle. Wrap the bare stems with a coordinating No. 9-width satin ribbon, from top to bottom to top again, leaving a "flag" of ribbon at the top.

LEFT:

Mothers-of-the-bride unanimously seem to be shying away from the standard pin-on corsages. And let's face it, the alternative wrist corsages are awkward at best. That explains the overwhelming trend of mothers choosing small nosegays or purse accents as their personal flowers.

how-to

Purse Flowers

136

Place a small strip of duct tape onto the outside of a purse, and glue foliage and flowers in corsage fashion to the tape with floral adhesive.

ABOVE:

To achieve the multidimensional color quality of this bouquet, three exquisite varieties of roses, in soft analogous hues, are expertly combined: the coral-orange 'Orange Unique'; the apricot-peach 'Versilia'; and the pale yellow 'Ambience,' which has coral-pink petal margins. Fresh *Magnolia* leaves, reversed to showcase the beautiful velvety brown color and texture of their undersides, further expand the autumnal harmony, and a perfectly coordinated plaid ribbon provides the ideal finishing touch.

For a captivating bride's bouquet that guests will remember, this collection of tulips, miniature callas, spray roses, and several types of orchids is assembled in an inverted bouquet holder to form a modified cascade. Long blades of bear grass flow from within the blossoms and add vertical movement to complete the cascading effect.

STEPHEN SMITH

An unmistakably autumn arrangement celebrates wedded bliss in the harvest season. Despite its natural hand-tied sheaf appearance, the wheat in this arrangement is actually cut in half, with the top and bottom halves of each stalk hot-glued into a floral-foam cage. 'Terra Cotta' carnations and a few preserved leaves are also arranged into the cage, and the arrangement is finished off with a bronze velvet bow.

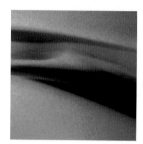

BELOW:
Yarrow adds a vibrant autumn color and texture to a nosegay-style arrangement of 'Circus' roses. Streamers of narrow golden-yellow velvet ribbon are a delightful alternative to the wide bows found on many floral badges.

how-to

Pew Wheat Sheaf

138

Cut stems of wheat 2 or 3 inches below the heads. Arrange the heads in one side of a small foam cage and the stems in the opposite side, to resemble a sheaf.

Arrange pieces of fresh foliage around the outside of the foam cage, being careful not to cover the heads of the wheat.

Arrange fresh carnations in a band across the center of the foam cage, and add a coordinating velvet bow underneath the carnations.

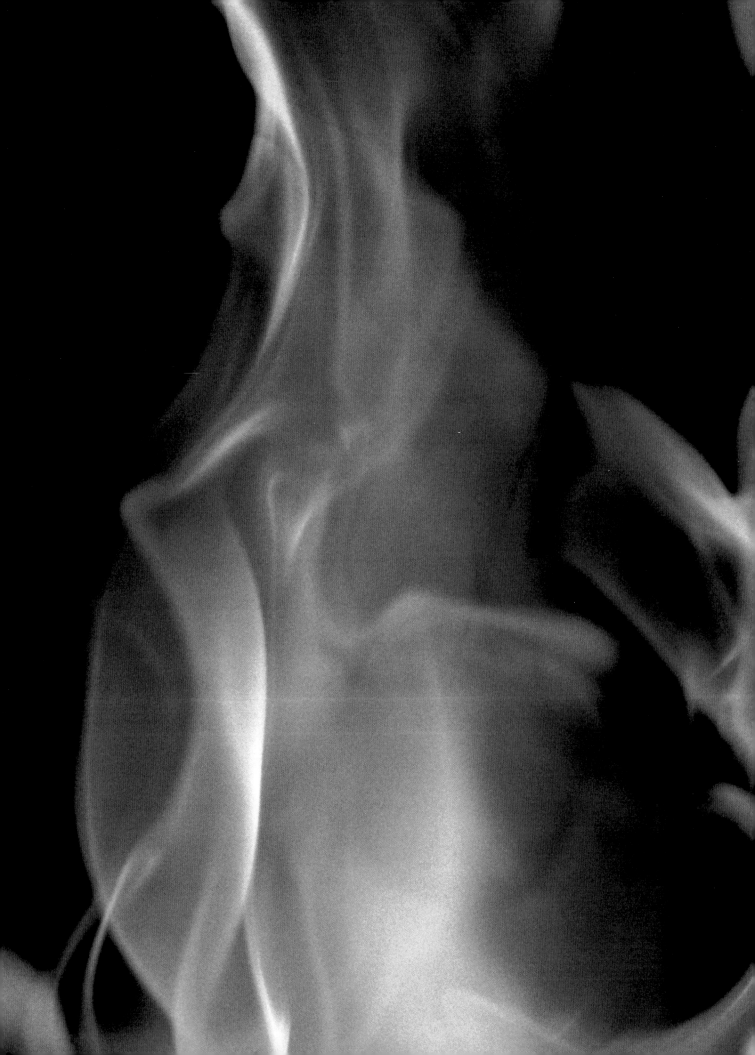

FLAME

Cattleya and *Cattleya* hybrid blossoms, in glorious reds, oranges, and yellows, are combined with creamy white *Phalaenopsis* blooms and a modicum of *Ruscus* foliage. A straight-handle bouquet holder is glued into a silver tussie-mussie, and the orchid stems are inserted directly into the foam.

FLAME SPIRITED **FIESTA** EMBER **INTENSE** BLAZE **RADIANT** CHILI **LUMINOUS** VIVID **BRILLIANT** SUN

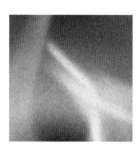

A simple, three-tiered cake is dressed up with a topper of multicolored roses in a silver mint julep cup and a coordinating wreath at the base. Instead of mixing the rose varieties, they are grouped by color in sections to create greater impact and draw attention to each variety.

ME SPIRITED **FIESTA** EMBER **INTENSE** BLAZE **RADIANT** CHILI **LUMINOUS** VIVID **BRILLIANT** SUNSET

STEPHEN SMITH

Defined by lush, exotic glory lilies (Gloriosa) and sweetly fragrant Freesias, this contemporary fall bouquet additionally features fresh Dahlias, yarrow, and Hypericum berries, all in vibrant autumnal hues. The florals are arranged in a bouquet holder nestled amid blades of lily grass (Liriope).

how-to

Grassy Weave Bouquet

144

Bundle several bunches of lily grass (Liriope), and bind them in two places, about 4 inches apart, near the bottom of the stems, with green waterproof tape.

Tape the straight handle of a bouquet holder with light-green stem wrap. Glue the holder into the center of the bundle of lily grass with floral adhesive.

Knot and tie together the ends of the blades of lily grass to form a decorative "grid"-like border to encircle the bouquet.

RIGHT:
Hand-tying is perhaps the preferred method for arranging delicate stemmed flowers such as the Iceland poppies *(Papavers)* and windflowers *(Anemones)* in this brightly colored nosegay. And even then, creating a support structure for the flowers is advisable, to hold them in place and prevent the delicate stems from breaking. In this bouquet, branches of 'Million Stars' baby's breath *(Gypsophila)* create just such an armature.

how-to
Gypsophila-Backed Nosegay

LEFT:
This free-form styling is the ideal arrangement for these captivating yellow-edged pinkish-red glory lilies *(Gloriosa)*, which have strongly reflexed petals. And the bamboo handle, which is formed by nestling a straight-handle bouquet holder into a cluster of 6-inch-long bamboo pieces, is the perfect accompaniment, providing additional allure and harmony. Shiny, dark-green *Camellia* leaves provide necessary contrast.

Arrange several stems of 'Million Stars' baby's breath into a loose nosegay in your hand.

Arrange delicate flowers like *Anemones* and poppies by inserting their stems through the baby's breath, allowing the baby's breath to support the blossoms.

Carefully wrap waterproof tape around the top of the bundle of stems so that the bouquet is held together but so that the stems are not crushed.

MARK ROBBINS

how-to

Royal Scepter

148

Using spray adhesive, glue fresh *Magnolia* leaves, brown sides out, to the backside of a straight-handle bouquet holder.

Cover the handle of the bouquet holder with waterproof tape, adhesive side out.

Adhere stems of heather, tips down, to the tape-covered handle. Bind the heather with beading wire to create a tapered "scepter." Glue *Magnolia* leaves to the grasping point on the handle to cover the ends of the heather stems.

LEFT AND OPPOSITE:
A truly grand creation fit for a queen, this bouquet features a stunning collection of blossoms, including glory lilies (*Gloriosa*), *Cymbidium* orchids, miniature *Cattleya* orchids, *Nerines*, and more. The materials are arranged into a straight-handle bouquet holder, the handle of which is gloriously elongated with wired heather to resemble a scepter.

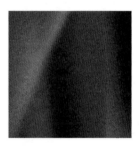

STEPHEN SMITH

ABOVE:
Cattleya and *Cattleya* hybrid blossoms, in glorious reds, oranges, and yellows, are combined with creamy white *Phalaenopsis* blooms.

POMEGRANATE

POMEGRANATE ROBUST **SENSUAL** VERMILION **FRUITY** TOMAT   ANGRIA VOLUPTUOUS S

MARK ROBBINS

BELOW:
To form this mixed flower bouquet, stems of like flowers are secured into small monobotanical bundles, then the bundles are gathered to form the final bouquet.

GRANATE ROBUST **SENSUAL** VERMILION *FRUITY* TO... ...CIOUS SANGRIA VOLUPTUOUS SPICY

OPPOSITE:
Available from California growers year-round, *Dahlias* are a wonderful—yet, perhaps, somewhat unexpected—choice for autumn weddings, when brides request a gardeny ambience. Traditional in style, this abundant mass bouquet of pretty pink and peach-colored blooms is designed in a romantic, classic pointed oval shape. A bouquet holder provides the required moisture for the flowers.

MARK ROBBINS

how-to
Magnolia Wrap Bouquet

154

This rich, colorful gathering composed of roses, miniature callas, *Nerines*, orchids, *Veronicas*, sea holly *(Eryngium)*, and more is arranged into a straight-handle bouquet holder, which is concealed by a wrapping of *Magnolia* leaves. The leaves are applied in an overlapping manner so that their brown backsides are visible.

Cover the foam cage of a bouquet holder with fresh *Magnolia* leaves, backsides out. Next, cover the handle with *Magnolia* leaves, in an overlapping manner, starting at the bottom, using larger leaves at the bottom and progressing to smaller leaves at the top.

Create a "garland" of folded *Magnolia* leaves (backsides out) by stitching along the fold with beading wire. Join the ends of the garland to form a wreath, which will be used to encircle the flowers.

Bend four lengths of heavy-gauge wire into "hairpin" shapes. Pierce the *Magnolia* wreath in four places with the wires, and insert the wires into the sides of the saturated bouquet holder. Arrange flowers into the bouquet holder.

OPPOSITE:
Recently "rediscovered" by style-conscious designers and consumers alike, carnations—especially the beautiful new variegated novelty varieties—create elegant, contemporary bridal bouquets and arrangements, particularly when arranged in mass.

RIGHT:
Equally lovely for brides and maids alike, this modern hand-tied bouquet showcases lush, gardeny florals arranged in sections for maximum exposure and impact. Frequently utilized as only a filler material, plume-like *Astilbe* is arranged as the dominant material while, conversely, roses, which are typically used as "feature" flowers, occupy a secondary role at the base of the *Astilbe*.

MARK ROBBINS

ABOVE:
Narrow feathers and thin strands of gold beading wire accent a sumptuous autumnal nosegay of miniature callas, *Gerberas*, English roses, sea holly (*Eryngium*), and *Anemones*.

how-to
Astilbe Sheaf Bouquet

Arrange stems of two bunches of *Astilbe* in hand, and bind the stems just under the blooms with stem wrap.

Arrange a row of roses around the base of the *Astilbe*, and tape them in place. Next add a "collar" of *Pittosporum* below the roses, and tape it in place.

Tie a two-loop bow with short streamers of wide, high-quality ribbon underneath the *Pittosporum*. Coordinate the colors of the ribbon with the flowers.

RIGHT:
Callas are perennial favorites of brides, regardless of the season, and miniature varieties are readily available in a number of hues that are appropriate for autumn weddings.

LEFT:
Narrow feathers and thin strands of gold beading wire accent a sumptuous autumnal nosegay of miniature callas, *Gerberas,* English roses, sea holly *(Eryngium),* and *Anemones.* A gold-plated bouquet holder adds glamour at an affordable price.

how-to

Tailored-Stems Bouquet

159

Individually wrap calla stems with No. 9-width silver organza ribbon, beginning at the base of each bloom, where the petal wraps over itself. Secure the ribbon at the bottom of each stem with floral adhesive.

Arrange the ribbon-wrapped callas into a bouquet, and bind the stems just below the blooms with several wraps of organza ribbon.

Secure the ribbon with gunmetal-colored pearl-head corsage pins at the binding point by pushing the pins into the stems.

LEFT:
Extra-wide ribbon, such as this peachy pink iridescent, quickly enwraps a cardboard disk, into which a hole is cut, to form a fashionable collar. The florals, a lavish collection of *Ranunculuses,* are arranged into a bouquet holder and dropped into the ribbon-wrapped collar. The various hues incorporated in the iridescent ribbon fabric coordinate perfectly with the sumptuous mound of multicolored blossoms.

how-to
Ribbon-Covered Disk

160

Cut a 10-inch-diameter disk from foam-centered board, and cut a hole in the center. Wrap the disk with No. 40 ribbon in an overlapping manner. Secure with corsage pins.

Wrap a bouquet holder handle with ribbon. Then, hot-glue and coil scrunched ribbon around the bouquet holder base from the center to the outer edge.

Insert the bouquet holder through the hole in the ribbon-covered disk and secure with hot glue. Arrange flowers and individual wired leaves into the holder.

ABOVE AND OPPOSITE:
Composed of a lavish profusion of orchids, including both *Dendrobium* and *Arachnis* (spider orchids), this fabulous arm bouquet would shine at any summertime celebration. With the addition of fern curls, the dramatic collection seems born of the rain forest.

TERRA COTTA

TERRA COTTA EARTHY **SUEDE** NUTMEG **MINK** CLAY **PERSIMMON** REAL **PAPRIKA** SEPIA **FAWN** BR

MARK ROBBINS

LEFT:
With its spiny, urchin-like florals, including a cluster of pincushions (*Leucospermum cordifolium*) and scarlet *Banksias* (*Banksia coccinea*), this exotic bouquet evokes images of the sea. The coordinating lei is made from hundreds of cigar flower blossoms (*Cuphea ignea*).

MARK ROBBINS

RIGHT:
Generally perceived as casual country blooms, sunflowers can be styled for sophisticated formal affairs as well. This moody hand-tied collection of black-dyed sunflowers is simple and elegant in design and style, and it would be magnificent for semiformal daytime or formal early evening ceremonies, especially against pale or neutral-colored gowns.

MARK ROBBINS

Just as if plucked from the bride's bouquet, this elegantly styled bouton-niere features a stem wrapped in sheer organza ribbon, which adds an air of formality and distinction as well as protection from staining.

RIGHT:
Two *Magnolia* leaves, folded so their backsides are visible, are bound together with beading wire to form a pocket-like holder into which a single blossom, such as the distinctive parrot tulip used here, may be dropped. In addition to its structural purpose, the pliable beading wire—when one end is fashioned into a small medallion—also serves a decorative purpose, accenting the regal boutonniere like a badge or miniature crest.

LEFT:
Designed with a fabulous bicolor 'Leonidas' rose and coconut-scented geranium leaves, this boutonniere is a princely selection for a fall event.

RIGHT:
Unquestionably autumn, this berried boutonniere features both *Cotoneaster*, with its golden-edged foliage, and bittersweet (*Celastrus*).

how-to
Lapel Pocket

167

Fold two *Magnolia* leaves in half, with backsides out. Place one leaf inside another to form a "V"-shaped "pocket." Pierce the base of the leaves with copper beading wire, and wrap the wire around the base to create a decorative band.

Make a small wad of beading wire, and flatten it to make a decorative "medallion." Wire the medallion onto the decorative wire band at the base of the leaves.

Glue a tulip (or a flower cluster of flowers of your choice) into the *Magnolia* leaf pocket with floral adhesive.

RIGHT:
An impressive autumnal bouquet is created with two simple elements— a straight-handled bouquet holder and a cardboard disk.

MARK ROBBINS

how-to
Asian Disk Bouquet

169

OPPOSITE:
Warm sunlight filtering through amber glass casts a golden glow onto this matching pair of altar pieces composed of English roses, *Gerberas*, parrot tulips, and fall foliages.

Cut a 10-inch- or 12-inch-diameter circle of cardboard. Cut a hole off-center to accommodate a straight-handle bouquet holder. Finish the backside with ribbon or fabric.

Glue assorted floral materials to the cardboard disk in a decorative, collage-like manner with spray adhesive. Trim florals with scissors to the shape of the disk.

Glue a small, saturated, straight-handle bouquet holder into the off-center hole in the disk with floral adhesive. Arrange flowers densely in the holder.

LEFT AND FAR RIGHT:
This hand-tied nosegay showcases autumn-colored 'Leonidas' roses, *Freesias,* and *Hypericum* berries combined with blue-violet *Eryngium* and *Ageratum* blossoms. A single large blue-green *Hydrangea* bloom is used as an "armature," or support mechanism, through which the other flower stems are arranged.

BELOW:
Woven of fresh Hawaiian palm, this jaunty hat, accented by a single red *Cattleya* orchid, is a playful accessory to fun-in-the-sun wedding celebrations.

how-to
Autumn Umber Nosegay

171

Arrange roses and *Freesias* though a single large *Hydrangea* blossom used as an armature. Bind the stems with green waterproof tape. The long stems will form the bouquet's handle.

Glue short-stemmed *Eryngium* and *Ageratum* blossoms and *Hypericum* berries into the *Hydrangea* blossom with floral adhesive.

With green waterproof tape, bind permanent *Magnolia* leaves to the underside of the bouquet to form a foliage collar. Conceal the tape with a wrapping of ribbon.

LEFT:
Featuring floating candles inside gold-dappled glass cylinders, these stylish creations are sure to add ambience to an evening reception. And with the stunning mix of colors and florals, they are suitable for either fall or Christmas events. Beneath the ornate iron trays, atop which rest gilded, permanent pears, a multicolored gathering of petals extends the designs onto the tabletop.

how-to
Gilded Cylinder

172

Spritz fresh ivy leaves with gold paint, spray them with adhesive, and press them onto a clay pot.

Fill a lined pot with floral foam, and attach a clear glass cylinder vase to the center of the foam with floral adhesive.

Spray gold metallic paint onto a piece of crumpled plastic and dab it onto the cylinder, creating a gilded look.

Florists' Review Enterprises, Inc.
www.floristsreview.com